THE COLOUR OF TIME

In memory of Barry O'Kelly
brother

Ring the bells that still can ring
Forget your perfect offering
There is a crack, a crack in everything
That's how the light gets in
– Leonard Cohen, *Anthem*

Úna Ní Cheallaigh

THE COLOUR OF TIME

ARLEN
HOUSE

The Colour of Time

is published in 2023 by

ARLEN HOUSE
42 Grange Abbey Road
Baldoyle
Dublin 13
Ireland
Phone: 00 353 86 8360236
arlenhouse@gmail.com
www.arlenhouse.ie

978–1–85132–303–6, *paperback*

Distributed internationally by
SYRACUSE UNIVERSITY PRESS
621 Skytop Road, Suite 110
Syracuse
NY 13244–5290
USA
Phone: 315–443–5534
supress@syr.edu
syracuseuniversitypress.syr.edu

Typesetting by Arlen House

cover image:
'The Seeker'
by Maria Noonan-McDermott
is reproduced courtesy of the artist

Contents

Acknowledgements

Acknowledgements are due to the editors of the following publications: *The Irish Times, Poetry Ireland Review, The Stony Thursday Book, The Quarry Man, Crannóg, Flare, Orbis, The North, Poetry Salzburg Review* and the Arlen House *Washing Windows* anthologies.

'The Letter' appears in *Washing Windows? Irish Women Write Poetry* edited by Alan Hayes (Arlen House, 2017)

'Suantraí' was shortlisted for *Poems for Patience* in 2019.

'Warrior Woman' was runner up in *Celebrating Women with Words* (2021), Circle Littéraire Irlandais, Paris.

I am deeply grateful to Poetry Circle at the Irish Writers Centre for a decade of collective support and forensic feedback, in particular the Pandemic Zoomers – Lynn Caldwell, Ben Keatinge, Maureen Daly, Joan Morrissey and Bill Dorris, hosted by Orla Martin.

Thanks are due to my early mentors, the poets Mary O'Donnell, Paula Meehan, John W. Sexton, Eileen Sheehan and Leanne O'Sullivan for their belief in my work. Very special thanks to Catherine Phil MacCarthy, James Harpur and Nessa O'Mahony for their endorsements, and for invaluable close reading and critical assessment of the manuscript in its many stages of development.

Much appreciation to my close companions in the craft, the late Larry Stapleton and Daragh Bradish. *The Colour of Time* is the richer for their constant support, wisdom and encouragement.

I am truly grateful for the support of family and friends, with special thanks to Monica O'Kelly and Éilis Collins.

Much appreciation and thanks to artist Maria Noonan-McDermott for her kind permission to use 'The Seeker' as the cover image. (www.marianoonan-mcdermott.com)

My sincere thanks to Alan Hayes of Arlen House for his confidence in taking on this collection and producing yet another beautiful book.

THE COLOUR OF TIME

MEMORIAL

GUST

The grey shed door has swung open
and, crazed pendulum, it beats
against the metal drainpipe.

The ash-barrel lid, now a rusted satellite
launched without warning,
trails ash from last night's fire

to spark into flame
the disturbed contents of two old tea chests:
telegrams, folded letters, opened, scattered,

become fragments, twisting into new patterns,
soon borne out of reach to a stranger's garden.
Secrets are burning –

first love's words left to smoulder, peat scented,
a boy's face blackened at the edges.
Into the evening sky
                    I watch a light journey out.

THE LETTER

Every day without fail he sends you a letter.
You put them all for safe keeping
in a satin pouch braided with gold cord,
corners looped like lovers' knots;
embroidered in chain stitch – your letter A.

On the morning after the assassination
of the Duchess and Archduke in Sarajevo:
Don't worry my dearest Annie, he writes,
sweetheart, it will surely come to nothing.

You put on hold the flood of telegrams
being sent from your switchboard
on behalf of the Empire;
fill the chamber of the Royal Mail's
fountain pen with black ink.

You ignore the lurch in your stomach,
respond to his foolish words of love.
You crumple the notepaper in your fist,
throw it like a dice on the chequered floor.

And by return of post you send to him
fondest sweet nothings, in Morse code.

FAMILY NOTICE
a found poem

Lance-Corporal Martin Rooney (4697),
5th Leinster Regiment, has been missing
since an engagement in France on the 13th May.

His mother will be very grateful for any
information his comrades can give her
through the Editor, *Evening Herald*.

SANCTUARY WOOD
i.m. Private Martin Rooney lost in action, Ypres, 12 May 1915

Only you know why you joined The Leinsters back then
and all we ever knew about you was your name.

The last address was a wood, southeast of Menin Road,
no letters sent – no one mentioned you were there.

Your war medal resting in the attic of 'Windele Road'
while you waited one hundred years at Menin Gate.

You were lost somewhere beyond the ridge at daybreak,
a devastated wood unable to give you sanctuary.

Crawling through darkness, the trench taken at bayonet point
that last night, no thought for enemy fire at dawn's light.

For you and all the missing, I will walk the Menin Road,
rest at 'Birr Cross Roads', they named from home,

then offer a simple prayer for all your comrades lost –

May a gentle breeze whistle through your wood
and saplings grow again covering scorched trees.
May ivy tendrils weave upwards toward the light
and white clover cover your body, bring you home.

MEMORIAL

With my finger I will trace your name,
bone touching stone at The New Menin Gate.
I will find you leaning against a scorched tree.

Just another Saturday afternoon, always the same
but the bells of Saint Mary's had stopped ringing.
She'd scrubbed the old floors of their rented rooms,
the two-pair front, in her own tin-pot way,
carried dirty water down to the yard.
She never spoke of what happened that day –
the crashing, the piercing screams, and her dread
racing up those rotting stairs. Praying, barely able
to call their names – the bed where they played
smashed under a fallen beam and Rose
huddled in the debris on the ground, the little ones
sheltered under her heaving chest,
crouching, protecting them under the safe roof
of her budding breasts. She saw the wolf in her.

INHERITANCE

In the week war in Poland began
the nuns laid her out
in Child-of-Mary blue,
mother of pearl rosary beads
between her fingers,
her nails,
domed and shaped to perfection,
painted a shade of oyster.

The Polish beautician holds my hands,
traces the contour
of each nail, feels its strength.
Beautiful, a gift, she whispers.
She chooses from her bottles
the oyster.
Then with her lacquered brush
she hides ten crescent moons.

SHE DREAMT OF ROSES

In the memorial garden on Île de la Cité
you'd easily miss, overwhelmed by Notre Dame,
roses not yet in bloom planted by deportees,
women from the camp at Ravensbruck.

The Resurrection Rose – a girl's dream
of a rose bouquet one winter's night;
she did not dream of a vermin
infested straw bed, her forgotten name.

That night she dreamt of roses –
this scented feeling of joy
like fresh water on her face
helping her forget mud-soaked feet;

long days of marching and longer days
yet to come, these mystical roses
bringing her beyond barbed wire;
a prisoner, she was free to dream.

(After Claudine Fourel – *Cette nuit, j'ai revé d'un bouquet de roses* –
Ravensbruck Camp, January 1945)

THE SCULPTOR'S LAST MENORAH
Nandor Glid, Thessaloniki, 1997

You stood at the lake's edge in winter
observing light fade to dark
on leafless trees lifting from the water,
a ghostly candelabra rooted deep –

your prayer for men forced to kneel
before a hostile crowd in Freedom Square,
dreams of milk and honey turned sour;
an incandescent star dyed yellow.

Branches scorched from Jesse's tree,
fifty thousand dead, now this menorah
once held to light the Sabbath
is how you shaped it yours –

fire rises from the ground,
bodies with open wings take flight.

ROSTROPOVICH PLAYS THE SARABANDE

And yet I play this cello for myself, in truth
the audience is only eavesdropping.
It is a souvenir, the music you hear behind that door,
a memory that escapes.

I play the Sarabande as if I am old;
an offering to those who feel sad, a prayer
for a lost child, an elegy for a country invaded.
And for you, my friend, may it be a safe haven.

Elena plays it now for me, her father;
I am still inside the music, a tear,
my last grace note slips and falls.
There is no need to wipe it away.

SOPHIE

Des femmes dans la photographie – Roger Moukarzel
Maison Européene de la Photographie, Ville de Paris

Of all the portraits yours is the one hiding
its secrets, a sculptured bird on the windowsill,
a talisman out of focus, not wanting to be seen.
I sit wanting to know you, study the detail.

You enter the gallery unaware that I am there
watching, and I am curious. It is you, Sophie,
stepping closer as if to look in a mirror.
I see you, the artist, walking away from that self.

SHOOTING EZRA POUND, GRESHAM HOTEL, 1965
i.m. Eddie Kelly, Irish Times

Not the photoshoot you expected
but perfect for you who loved to be still.

Portrait of a poet who refused to speak,
a silent subject, not lying in state
but sitting in a foyer waiting to leave.

No questions to be asked – that was his way and yours –
holding back in stillness with an open Leica lens,
slow catlike, your one eye focused on his face,
listening as he for that crucial line break.

You draw the eye to look,
see in profile a grey-haired man
gazing beyond the frame, shoulders hunched.

You pull us in deeper and deeper still,
into the lines of his bearded face,
looking for what's unsaid.

All the dark weight sinking down
like an old galleon on your shore
waiting for that perfect angle,
that light connecting image,
to capture more than passing ships,
to wait,
          yes wait
                    for Cantos sung in silence.

THE GLASS EYE

When told you had a glass eye
I searched my marble jar
for one that looked like yours –
pale blue, opaque,

imagining you every night placing
this moonlike sphere on a walnut
table crafted with inlaid veneer,
then like an ancient Cyclops sleeping,

your camera always by your side,
never out of sight. *But why?*
You only need one eye, you'd wink.
I'd laugh, pretend I understood.

In the *Irish Times* the other day
your photograph re-appears –
Bloomsday 1982 – Jorge Luis Borges
in an armchair in The Shelbourne Hotel –

hands resting on a polished walking stick,
blindness and age worn lightly behind that smile;
light falling on his face in shadowplay –
his left eye sparkling mischief.

BENEDICTUS

I am waiting at the five-road junction
for traffic lights to change,
the stadium dome has disappeared

and Shelbourne Road is tree-lined
as it was a century ago.

Standing at a different angle
a world can disappear

and Joyce is writing love letters to Nora
in number sixty's upstairs room.

From here in June he leaves to meet her
on a Dublin strand,
                        his Nora,
                                Nora Barnacle.

A vixen crosses my path, side glances me –
            a death,
                    a blessing from Molly B.

IN THE WINGS

Waiting for house lights to come down,
feeling our adrenalin rise, watching each other closely,

the two of us, washerwomen wrapped in shawls
counting seconds to blackout
and our cue to move unseen downstage.

Lights up!

We are on our knees on the banks of Anna Livia Plurabella
scrubbing the parson's drawers in syncopated rhythm
throwing the opening lines across an apron stage –

Did you hear? Did you where?

And we're off at a mad mare's gallop
flipping and flapping across imaginary waves
spreading our washing, tossing our words –

Wring out the clothes! Wring out the dew!
Will we spread them here now? Aye we will. Flip!

We dance the wake, sing the songs, spin
each other round, tell the tale of Shem and Shaun –

Tell me Tell me Tell me elm ...
Lord help you, Maria, full of grease,
the load is with me!

Waiting in the wings for your last appearance
I let the hearse pass by,
stand at the gate as you enter the grounds
and you are carried centre stage

and I want to sing –
just a song at twilight when the lights are low
softly in the shadows ...

the show must go on
and Anna Livia will wind her way past Eve and Adam.

BRECHT'S LAST HOUSE

He's sitting
at a worn desk by the window
looking down on Chausséestrasse
and the cemetery beyond

writing no more epic plays but poetry
his first love,
once again back in Berlin in this house
where life would end
closing his own *chalk circle*

and this

his afterlife
a desk, a chair, an old typewriter,
objects that no one dares to touch

a simple life
among four thousand books.

The Caucasian Chalk Circle by Bertolt Brecht, 1898–1956

LIFE DRAWING

How she chose to die is her secret,
alone all those years living in New York,

no need to say a word, not a single word
but remember giggling schoolgirls
sitting still for hours, posing for portfolios

and she insisted I untie my waist-length hair,
laughing at her own mousy page boy cut –
let it blow free, it's art for art's sake.

My portrait was unseen until the last brush stroke
and she unveiled a Pre-Raphaelite, radiant,
wearing white, folds of golden hair hiding

half her face, the hazel eyes were mine
but the mirror was not cracked –
no painted prow, no web, no loom

just a simple wooden boat
and the Lady of Shalott floating
by tangled reeds toward Camelot.

RECITAL
While through the sense your song shall fit
The soul to understand.
– 'Song and Music', Dante Gabriel Rossetti

In the Church of the Holy Archangels
I notice how she follows with grace
the ensemble to the highest altar,
her Baroque violin held close.

A Rossetti, pale luminous skin, long
waves of hair clasped at her neck;
a muse chosen to fulfil desire, her song –
an aching pulse of melodies.

Her stillness, her breath rising, then falling
to the music. Soloist, she now steps forward
as if called to take a sacred place and she is lost,
listening for the unwritten word inside each note.

If he, Dante Gabriel, heard her play,
eyes closed, fingers blessing each string,
he would be compelled to paint invisible wings;
consumed, he would not see his feet aflame.

Trattoria Pietra Martire

We sit facing the river at Ponte Pietra.
The waiter describes in detail the *Fish of the Day* –
La Orata, gilt-headed
with a dry white from the region –
Soave, light and delicate.

Do you understand? you ask.
Sparus Aurata, sea bream.
Words float as I catch meaning,
a subliminal soakage,
full of strange phrases from arias –

Laschia ch'io pianga, mia crude sorte
drifts to the surface,
Let me weep, my cruel fate, my reply.
The fish has been gutted and boned,
lies perfect on the plate.

Do you remember the film *Farinelli?*
You find the aria for me on YouTube.
I laugh, *Fish and Farinelli,* and then stop.
The castrato in gilded headdress sings
Laschia chi'o pianga, mia cruda sorte

A young boy is held in a bath,
his blood weeping into water.

A FAREWELL TO GRIEF AT LAGO MAGGIORE

Like Electra I carry grief on my shoulder,
a weight, always there, unseen,
colouring each day with tinges of grey.
Wanting to heal what I cannot name
I return to these lake waters where Hemingway
rowed nightly to Pescatori, for him
the island that *beat paradise all to hell,*
fishermen guiding his way through darkness.

The swans are here nesting in the shelter of the quay,
their slow glide at sunset, a whiteness more pristine
than the Pallazo reflected in the lake's pink hue.
Sitting by this lake with glass in hand, thoughts slip
and slide, a penny for them? Iced caramels.
I crave sweetness, dolce – *la dolce vita.*

MÉMOIRE DE MONTDEVERGUES

In memory of Anita Readman
artist

THE SECRET

As if there were no words,
just cold white marble pressed against palms;

as if you wanted to say we clasp this secret,
like the unborn child we never held;

as if our fingertips barely touching
showed what passed between us;

as if the clay of Montfavet would be enough
to make me nameless.

(after *Le Secret by* Auguste Rodin)

MEMORIAL STONE

CAMILLE CLAUDEL
1864–1943
SCULPTOR
LIVED AND WORKED IN THIS BUILDING
ON THE GROUND FLOOR FROM 1899 TO 1913
BY WHICH DATE HER SHORT CAREER AS AN ARTIST
ENDED
AND THE LONG NIGHT OF HER INTERNMENT
BEGAN

'THERE IS ALWAYS SOMETHING ABSENT WHICH
TORMENTS ME'

(LETTER TO RODIN, 1886)

19 Quai de Bourbon
from Camille's letters

I paid the carter with what little money I'd left.
Headless torsos, shattered limbs – a life's work
for nothing, taken away on a horse-drawn cart.
In the moment I grasped the claw hammer,
I knew this act would haunt me to my grave.
By night I walked the quay, throwing last fragments
in the Seine, the river disturbed, stillness broken;
such deeds would count for madness in their eyes.
Interned, I am growing old, and like that man
sitting at *eternity's gate,* sadness bears me down.

(*Eternity's Gate* by Vincent Van Gogh (1853–1890) / Saint Rémy de Provence, 1890)

ASYLUM
from Camille's letters

I have fallen into a void, a nightmare.
The dream that was my life –
so curious, so strange. Another Eve,
banished, hidden out of sight, out of mind.
I touched their nakedness, but it was not lust,
clay was my passion, my desire, yet always
something missing that tormented me.

What was my crime! To be Camille?
I am like a Donkey Skin, a Cinderella
condemned to keep the ashes of the heart.
No one there to change these clothes of skin
and ash into dresses the colour of time. How
can you sleep so soundly while so many
women shout – Help, I am drowning?

* Montdevergues Asylum, Montfavet

To Eugène Blot

Times when it's so hard I cannot bear it –

I rub stale bread between my fingers,
feel the curve of cold tin plates,

my hands longing for clay to mould the pain,
to cast their vacant eyes, their bitten nails.

I gave my hands, my young body to Rodin,
you'll find them burning at *The Gates of Hell*.

* Eugène Blot (1857–1938), gallery and foundry owner
The Gates of Hell by Auguste Rodin (1840–1917)

FROM MONTDEVERGUES TO PAUL CLAUDEL

What joy if I could find myself at Villeneuve again?
Remember those nights when we stole out into woods,
climbed the massive rocks to *The Devil's Hood*;

you gave a name to every shadow the moonlight
threw on stones; imagine now if your words
were stolen, no paper, no pen, never a line spoken –

All your work for nothing, and no one to applaud.

---

* Paul Claudel (1868–1955) – dramatist, poet, Camille's brother
  La Hotteé du Diable near Villeneuve

MA MÈRE

I did not sense her death
and when I try to find

one beam of recollection,
there is nothing.

I will not allow bitterness
to haunt me here,

fifteen years and more
without seeing her face.

My love of clay, my love of him,
always that wall between us

and she is committed now
to earth, my chosen mother.

The keeper rakes the soil, smooths
its surface before the darkness comes.

So many days without light
yet I can see the changing skies,

imagine myself walking
beyond these asylum walls

or forever in that fireside dream
raking burnt embers and ash.

* *Fireside Dream* by Camille Claudel
private collection, dated 1895–1905

JESSIE'S VISIT, MONTDEVERGUES 1929

Silence when she left.

My only hope, her promise
to tell the world that I am sane;
we laughed like the girls we were

in those Colarossi days, drinking
English tea from Jessie's china cups
in our studio in Notre-Dame-des-Champs.

She helped me remember what I chose
to forget, the London exhibition
at the Royal, her terracotta piece

called *Sans Soucie* and the plaster
portrait of me she wrapped
in her mother's best damask cloth

for fear that I might break.

She spoke with gentle words
of broken dreams, how she found
love back then and I could not.

She'd tell the world that I'm not mad,
let them see that they are wrong.
But will they listen?

* Jessie Lipscomb and Camille Claudel trained together at Académie
Colarossi, Paris in 1882. Lipscomb exhibited work in the Royal
Academy London in 1887.

L'ÀGE MÛR

To mark this moment your husband took our photograph.

We are sitting together, our backs to crumbling
plaster, neglected, needing a sculptor's touch.

Just given the chance what we would have done with it.

This image will outlive us, two women
of mature age, but what will the eye see?

One with eyes open looking at him behind the lens,
and the other, her dulled windows without light.

Would they even notice who was free?
Who was not?
                    If only, if only I

could once more sculpt this reflection I see
in rainwater, for there are no mirrors here,

it would be what I imagined then, the face
of the old woman I'd held between my hands.

L'Àge Mûr/The Mature Age by Camille Claudel (various 1895–1913)

LA VAGUE

I managed to hold back this ocean

until my only visitors had gone
but now the waves resurge

unable to find sleep, even a little rest

this life of loneliness
my mother's only bequest

and all that's left will be found
forgotten on the shore

comme les trois destins

young women dancing naked
beneath the swell of blue onyx green

their bodies golden.

La Vague/The Wave by Camille Claudel (1897–1903)
Les Trois Destins/The Three Fates

The Last Medusa

I am still holding the hammer,
hearing its first blow, fury
as her head crashes to the floor,

shattering like a quake
through all these losses,
doors closed, work uncast.

Afraid to look the gorgon in the eye,
he kept his back turned to me,
the invisible mirror held by its shaft,

snake tendrils crawling at my feet.
I struck the final blows of obliteration,
my body, my mind, all lost in rising dust.

Perseus and the Gorgon by Camille Claudel (1902), her last sculpture

TRIPTYCH

not a beginning
a middle
an end
      but a shifting
I cannot separate or tear apart
a young girl's dreams
from all that followed
like plaster light to the touch
changing to white marble's sheen
and now this darkness cast in bronze

SAKUNTALA

I was foolish back then
I believed in magic spells –
separated lovers re-uniting

Sakuntala, Sakuntala

forever in her lover's arms
I placed her head gently
resting on his forehead

his upturned face
against her cheek
always kneeling before her

and they are one
how I wanted to show their love
hoping it would be enough.

(Sakuntala /plaster 1886)

VERTUMNUS AND POMONA

Time says
call him by another name

Vertumnus
how he could seduce

All I did not see
such trickery!

I allowed him into my orchard
watched the seasons change

He took all he desired
my ripest golden fruit

And I like Pomona
silent

No!
I could never be ...

(Vertumnus and Pomona, marble 1905)
(Sankuntala sculpture re-worked and re-named)

L'ABANDON

I left him
to go beyond those shadows

A lover's gaze
no longer at my feet

I abandoned illusion
cast my dream in bronze

No longer Sakuntala
no longer Pomona

Moi, je suis
                    Camille Claudel

(*L'Abandon,* bronze 1905)

CHIAROSCURO

In memory of Larry Stapleton
poet

WARRIOR WOMAN
for Eileen O'Mahony

I saw the sun's disc throw slatted light
on towels you left on the bathroom floor,
the shower wheelchair dripping on black sacks.

I heard the motor's purr,
its smooth glide along the hallway –

the neighbour's blue-eyed cat
rubbing its sleek coat against the open doorway
entered before you

and on your lap
grape hyacinth and daffodils
barely opened,
the spring's first offerings –

you put the flowers on the windowsill
and as you made a perfect turn
spokes became golden –

your restlessness, sleepless nights, endless
counting of stars, all those moons
shadowed for a moment by the sun,

amber like bolts of fire
around your neck,
a goddess guiding your chariot
through all your battles,

host to the fallen,
protected by your feathered cloak
you shifted shape
flying like a falcon in dreams.

FIRE CIRCLES

crow women dream
       paint their claws
              in dotted circles

children trace their footprints
       dream lost stories
              burnt feathers, stolen fire

tourist shops sell their past
       Fairtrade
              for coloured dots

must hide the sacred
       no secrets
              to be sold

fathers in Freemantle
       serving time
              paint on cell walls

whitewashed bricks too pale
       need red earth
              to show their fire

a woman from a distant tribe
       remembers the *cailleach*
              and the crone

sits before dawn by bush fire
       waits for sunrise
              over Uluru

THE STOLEN
for an Aboriginal child

And in her sleep she hears
a grandmother call her name,

a name she knows, but dare not speak.

Leave the city that has stolen you,
the begging and the drinking.
Leave the dealing and the heroin,
the gang fights and the scars.

*

And in her sleep she hears
a sister call her home

to a place she remembers, but never saw.

Come back to your desert path,
to your language, to your people.
Come back to the red mountain,
the bush fire and the painted caves.

*

And in her sleep she hears
a lost child sing the words

for family, the tribe she never knew.

Come sit with the wise women in their circle,
their healing and their dreaming.
Come sit with your children by the flame trees,
gather wild honey and wattle seeds.

*

And in her heart she hears
her birthmother tell her story,

whisper her skin name.

NEEDLEWORK

You scoured Hickey's bargain basement
for a remnant of Japanese shot silk;
winged patterns of jade, lapis lazuli,
vermilion blossoms cool against skin.

I admired the cushions you made,
envied you your skill –
(a lift in mood, euphoric in hindsight).

The night before, we ate Turkish Delight,
drank tea from tulip glasses
I'd brought from Istanbul.

How come I didn't notice –
catch the subtext in the pause –
the part you played and I was convinced.
(The detailed plan already made).

I search for traces of a scene
I can't bear to imagine,
trying to unpick what I missed.

I find cushions
neatly placed on your bed,
bias-binding ribbons loosely tied.
Kenzo floral lost in Dettol's heavy smell.

Specks of blood like pinpricks on the rug –
all traces of pills, booze, Gillette blades
cleared away.

I sit out the crucial days waiting
for the hospital to ring.
Wander in rooms,
searching for remnants.

When I visit
you show me wrists
stitched with black silk thread.

IN A DREAM MY MOTHER'S FACE APPEARS

floating in water from a recess so deep
that I wonder is it true
or just a strange story I tell myself and yet
the child is me and she is there

lifting me up to paint with her at a table
covered with old newspapers –
I am wearing my painting pinny
and she has rolled up my sleeves

she steadies my hand to fill jam jars
from the water jug – one to wet
and one to rinse those sable brushes –
I paint animals in cages, she adds markings

stripes and sharp teeth to bring my zoo to life
she leans towards my picture
I see two faces looking at me through jars
my dipped brush turns one to murk

the smiling face is barely opaque
and she becomes a double image
moving in darkening waves
I reach across to stop her face

shifting in dark distorting glass
with a fist I knock the jars
drowning our painted world
her smile sinking under water

MY MOTHER'S BONE MARROW

We make light of it as we sit on a high
hospital bed our feet unable to touch ground

unsure of what will happen next
trying to pretend there's nothing wrong

but the intern's face says it all
and you and I can see he is afraid

the nurse does not look at us but checks her watch
time's face turned upside down

a covered needle on a stainless tray
its length impossible to conceal

I'm asked to leave as she pulls the faded curtain
closing you in – I want to stay

you let me go with words of a poem
you've always known by heart –

the shade of his hand – you say
in a voice so low I want to plead

implore your hound from heaven
to hold you gently between his paws

suck the marrow from your bones
stroke his fur against your punctured spine

calm with holy saliva your burning skin
then pour his animal spirit on every bruise
and lie down with you in the drifting snow

(*The Hound of Heaven* by Francis Thompson, 1859–1907)

WILD STRAWBERRIES

You take each one by its needle stalk,
hold midsummer berries up to natural light,
blood-red like platelets that drip into your veins,

discard the bruised and over ripe;
inhale fruit-picking flapper days,
those carnival flings in fields near Rush.

And you find buried deep the smallest one,
offer its young blush to me to taste –
I bite and juice dribbles down my chin.

In a rogue swoop you wipe the truant
drops clean, raise a red-tipped talon
to moisten your sun-parched lips.

THE CELLIST
for Aisling Drury Byrne, Mater, Eccles Street, 1982

Daughters and strangers, never speaking
on the way to our mothers' rooms.
These last days – hospital visits – intermezzo
in rehearsal routine, your cello always by your side.

Your vigil over but mine going on,
I am urged to take some rest
from sounds of death rattling the air

and I can nearly forget why I'm here
lying on a vacant bed in the small hours
sensing your mother dying here this morning,
now peaceful in the morgue below.

I lie on her deathbed staring at a white ceiling rose,
the satin eiderdown skin cold,
listening for strains of music that filled her life.

Did you hear a faint cry as you played *Saint Saens,*
calling you to be with her in this soft nest,
feathers hiding a lifeless wing?

Playing *andantino grazioso* with swan's grace –
you listen for the sigh, hold a weightless final note.

Le Cigne/The Swan for cello by Saint-Saens (1835–1921)

EURYDICE'S HUSBAND

It's possible I sang
before I followed you to our grave.
Some say I followed out of fear.
That I didn't have the courage or heart
to go on without you.
But you know that's not true.
The day the serpent bit into the marrow,
sucked your blood,
there was little choice.
I trailed its deadly crawl.
It was not dead or alive, simply creeping
between our worlds.
I leaned across your body
into folds of starched sheets.
My head lightly resting,
I touched your thinning hair,
listening for the breath
                    trapped in our throats.
Wanting to kiss you, to bring you home,
because I didn't know what else to do,
I followed in despair.
It was the serpent re-appearing hissing at me,
remission like rotten fruit between its fangs.
You left our silver marriage coins
on the bedside locker,
your silence broken
by Charon's dog howling in corridors.
I cut strings with my teeth,
left wood for kindling.

(After Wislawa Szymborska)

GHOST PARADE

Maybe it's the sound of ghosts drumming
that makes me count the days since you died;
lost in a chanting crowd with faces white as mine
wanting to dye my hair sickly green, wear black lipstick.

I look for you among the painted ghosts, makeshift coffins –
the dead's trappings – carnival songs beating winter's end
in chilled breaths along the Rhine. Too soon for spring.
Yet revellers pay no heed, vow to greet a frozen dawn.

Song birds won't sing in hard weather but will follow
the call to fly south in their time
and your forty days staying close have passed.
I can no longer hear the sound of your voice.

FASNACHT

There were no pancakes no Mardi Gras
just roasted bratwurst and beer
and a straw man hanging on the pub door
waiting for Ash Wednesday
and the carnival nearly over
crowds spilled out on to cobbled streets
a Rhymer standing on a barrel
shouted words I did not understand
mocking incantations turning into song
I was holding a stranger's hand
dancing to accordion music
stamping to the drumbeat
cheered when the Nübbel
was torn down and set alight
I danced around the burning man
in circles spinning faster and faster
my dulled senses blazing into life
the stranger spun me round and round
the burning embers and I was singing
joining in the chorus rhyming
like a caged wren leaving her feathers at an open door.

No Love Lost

I see you first,
sitting alone in Starbucks
staring into dark-roasted froth.

You lift your gaze,
a moment's slip in your reflection
watching me pay for an Americano
and my wish to be invisible evaporates.

Always the charmer
you insist I join you
and I am caught yet again
like a snake coiled in dark
folds of jute sacking.

I listen to a one hour show with the latest
updates of your successful life
and you throw the usual closing line –

How are you doing? –
as you glance at your iPhone,
check the time.

I catch the familiar look –
I really don't need to know,
pick up the purse you gave me
and you smile,
comment on my perfume –
(*Calvin Klein,* your gift from Duty Free)

Still the same?
Yes, still the very same.

I hear the coffee machine hiss
as I push a glass door out to the street,

feel its heavy swing behind me,
breathe in fumes
more potent than *obsession*.

WINTER JASMINE

It is still October yet the Winter Jasmine
impatient, has appeared. Solitary flower,
its yellow hidden among fading leaves,
others will follow, no longer waiting
for the solstice to announce their time;
to be seen naked on bare stems, star bright
petals needing little light. Has she lost
her timing or is this confusion the game we play?

SOLSTICE

All that winter I waited.
I knew you would go before the solstice.

And you did, you left just as the sun
was finding its way

into the chamber at Newgrange.
I see you walking the valley

to the stone cairn,
its grassy mound always a surprise;

white quartz gleams
as you pass through the open doorway.

Stone by stone, along the damp passage,
you are led into its womb,

your shadow cast.
It was strange how it was nearing the end;

the carers dressed you in red, not your colour,
for the Christmas party,

Jingle Bells, crackers and Baileys Irish Cream.
And as you were spun around the floor

you smiled, and smiled back at them,
the sun's secret in your pocket.

DEORA DÉ

Let it be the way it is, let it fall
the wind-blown fuschia
lets go another tear

remember how she disappeared
under the heavy weight of thaw
a snowslide

left her damaged
bruised branches torn apart
her last season

slowly in her secret way
she appeared in new robes
one for every occasion

'and you thought I was a lost cause!
under the snow I returned to my roots
buried in black peat and terracotta

I left the world
dreamed deeper shades of purple, blood reds
found why you call me by this name.'

* *Deora Dé/God's tears* – Irish name for Fucshia

NOCTURNE

Sleep – you took it with you.
So many nights I've longed to close my eyes,
drift at last into dream. I do not blame

you for robbing me of rest, you have given
stillness – silent hours waiting
for day to slowly break through the skylight;

a welcome chorus of birdsong, drowned by gulls
screeching in flight as they leave the strand,
a foghorn beyond the lighthouse at Poolbeg

and your last dawn when the ice-moon
was on the verge of waning, a fox crossing
the hospice carpark its tail barely touching

bold white lettering on black tarmac
guiding you, marking your exit.

SUANTRAÍ

Brent geese leave the island at high tide
to feed on the green beyond your door

I see you little one for the first time
home after weeks in detox

your mother asks me to take you in my arms
heroin's trace still creeping in your veins

your face pale
drained beyond hunger

watchful eyes take me in
I hear wildcat cries

haunting your sleep

and forgotten words of a lullaby –
seoithín seó uilleó ló

I place my hand close to your heart
seoithín seó 's tú mo leanbh

massage your breath into gentle circles
seothín seó 's tú mo mhaoin

slowly the feral cry subsides

a little beak grips
you suck my finger

my goose girl with the ebbing tide
flies back to her salt marsh to feed.

ABOUT THE AUTHOR

photograph © Stephanie Joy

Úna Ní Cheallaigh was born in Dublin. Educated at St Patrick's College (DCU), University College and Trinity College Dublin, she had a varied career in teaching, including Special Education, Home School Community Liaison and Drama in Education.

A love of theatre led to her pursuing an M. Phil in Theatre Studies at Glasgow University. She has been involved in drama and writers' groups and is currently a member of Poetry Circle at the Irish Writers Centre. She was conferred with a Masters in Creative Writing (University College Cork) in 2017.

She has enjoyed many opportunities to travel, attend literary festivals and workshops in Australia, Scotland, and Wales. Time to write in Ferrazze, Italy, was organised by the Irish Writers Centre. A month spent in Paris, staying at the Centre Culturel Irlandais (2018), gave rise to the sequence at the heart of *The Colour of Time,* giving voice to the sculptor, Camille Claudel. Poems from 'Mémoire de Montedevergues' were performed at Bray Literary Festival, 2020.